MW01245154

For Love of Country

For Love of Country

Common Sense 2.0

NORMAN W. HOLDEN

ISBN 978-1-7362203-6-8 (eBook)
ISBN 978-1-7362203-7-5 (Paperback Edition)
ISBN 978-1-7362203-8-2 (Hardcover Edition)

Library of Congress Control Number: 2023908992

Book cover and interior design by C'est Beau Designs

Printed and bound in the United States of America
First printing 2024

Published by NWH Holdings, LLC
Colorado, USA

www.normanholdenbooks.com

POL046000 POLITICAL SCIENCE / Commentary & Opinion

This book is dedicated to the future of America.
May her ideals weather the test of time, and may she
withstand the transgressions of human interference.

Contents

Preface

If freedom of speech is taken away,
then dumb and silent we may be led,
like sheep to the slaughter.

—GEORGE WASHINGTON

Those freedoms bestowed by our Creator, thoughtfully and eloquently framed within the First Amendment of the United States Constitution by the Founding Fathers, allow me to offer the following words without fear of being silenced.

With this obligatory qualification out of the way, let us now address the elephant (or donkey) in the room. What you are about to read will not sit well with many in power or their supporters. Detractors will immediately try to vilify, label, or place this book and me in a box. Most likely, I will be titled a "nationalist," "far-right conspiracist," or some other diversionary term. Predictably, those who do will, without haste, diagnose me with a multitude of phobias all in an effort to marginalize my voice or alter the narrative. It is difficult to describe the status of our modern-day existence or provide a meaningful warning without offending or upsetting a portion of our society. Regrettably, this is what America has become: a polarized society of "us" versus "them." Thus, we have deliberately been plunged back into tribal groups.

My tone, and the content for which I intend to explore, will admittedly strike a nerve for many readers. Many of my fellow Americans on the left may wholeheartedly disagree with some of my points. While my words may seem antagonistic, I respectfully implore my fellow Americans to override the urge to dismiss this editorial and see this experiment to its end. The topics for which I challenge affect all Americans, and only *We the People* can correct our course.

I want to be clear for the reader: You may label me anything you choose; however, your words will not hurt me. Thankfully, I was raised in the era of "sticks and stones"[1]; therefore I can handle it. In the end, I would prefer to be called an American. I will not shrink away or apologize for this statement. Fortunately, and by no choice of my own, I was born and raised in this country. I am truly grateful for the blessings that have been bestowed upon this land and its citizens. While I have no supreme authority to do so, I accept her "from sea to shining sea,"[2] warts and all. However, I am confident that if we all did the same, our country would be in a much better position. Unfortunately, as a nation and a civil society, I feel we are teetering on the edge of a dangerous precipice, and that is the catalyst behind this book. These remarks are put forth in favor of and love for America.

This book is not intended to be a dog whistle for one side of the aisle or the other. Rather, it was intentionally written and meant for all Americans, for those who believe that the original plan for our nation was meant to be a force for good. My words are aimed at those Americans who love our country and feel we have lost our way and strayed off course into a storm of polarization, defeatism, and loathing for the land of the free. This book is for those who are concerned about our future and the breakdown of our social fabric and overall decline of our nation. If you dislike America and approve of the current anti-American narrative, agree with censorship, like to modify history or the facts, think good citizenship is divisive and/ or traditional American values are racist, then prepare to be triggered.

If I sound defensive, I am. My perspective stems from a deep sadness and frustration with the ongoing degradation of our country and civil society. My words are overburdened by a broken heart. My deep reverence for our nation and its citizens brings forth a passioned retort that at times may sting or come across as a superior viewpoint. Please understand that I am merely a humble servant delivering difficult news that should be heeded.

This book is my second chance to do what I feel is owed to our great nation. Due to health reasons, I was disqualified from serving our country in military uniform. Consequently, I feel indebted to our nation and to those who sacrificed for our freedom. I recognize that this gesture does not measure up to the sacrifices our men and women in uniform offer up on a daily basis, nor does it carry the same level of risk that Thomas Paine and the many other Founding Fathers endured, yet this is my contribution. Consider it one patriot's tithe to his fellow Americans—past, present, and future.

I feel obligated to provide a similar provision, as I wrote in my first book titled *Do Better!*, where I convey that I am not a therapist, licensed professional, counselor, academic, theologian, or historian. Also, I am not a sheep blindly being led to slaughter. I am, however, like many in this great nation, an everyday man, a husband, and a father of three. I am an American. Like my homeland, I am a tarnished vessel. My blue-collar roots are richly planted and were nourished by the American spirit. I, like millions of others, have benefited from this great nation. I have simply hit my limit of negativity, self-loathing, and the constant bombardment of haters putting America down. She deserves much better.

There are many great patriots of all walks of life, from the beginning until now. Thankfully, I am in very good company. Like the patriots of our past, I am no better than my fellow citizens, and I own no moral high ground. Admittedly, I am not an authority on the subject matter on which I write. Yet as a patriot grounded in the soil of the American ethos, I can no longer silently stand by and allow the erosion of our country and freedoms. As a citizen and a fellow steward of American values, I have a duty to protect what was bestowed upon us by much nobler men and a higher power.

I'm not claiming to be an original thinker as it relates to many of these thoughts and theories; I am simply trying to consolidate from a common man's perspective what many of us in America are experiencing. While my views are not unique, I cannot stand idly by and allow the acts of betrayal against the American people to continue.

I could have easily kept my thoughts to myself, as many with similar views do out of fear of reprisal. However, until the American people stand up and fight for their rights, the likelihood that we are enslaved by those who wish us harm will only strengthen. Unable to bear this injustice, I share my beliefs with the hope of rejuvenating the spirit of Paine's *Common Sense*.

Finally, I wish to dispel any thoughts that this is a callous manifesto issued by a martyr in support of a political party or candidate. Instead, it is one man's thoughts on the decline of America. I am neither publicly supporting or endorsing a candidate or political affiliation, nor am I seeking political office. While this book is political in nature, it is the author's opinion that this is a national issue that should concern all the citizens of the republic. I am humbly expressing my sincere cautionary advice on what I feel is best for the good people of our country. I publish this public warning for the citizens of this great nation only out of love, gratitude, and the hope for a better America.

A House
Divided

*If destruction be our lot, we must ourselves be
its author and finisher. As a nation of freemen,
we must live through all time, or die by suicide.*

—ABRAHAM LINCOLN

Tribalism is the preferred weapon of choice. I firmly believe we are intentionally being torn apart from the inside out. There are evil forces at work striving to obtain ultimate power over the American people and our nation. It was once stated that "A great civilization is not conquered from without until it has destroyed itself from within."[3] If tribalism is the instrument of destruction, then complacency and a steady overfed diet of fear are the chinks in our armor.

Instead of cultivating cooperative behavior and common values, we are slowly becoming more tribally biased and irrational. We are losing empathy and trust for those outside our prescribed ideological groups and party labels. Neither side is willing to look for compromise. Instead, we gather in defensive postures and shift into attack mode. Like it or not, *We the People* are being played. Through our complacency we have become a worn-out broken instrument, now out of tune with missing and broken strings. We have become a "house divided against itself,"[4] which will not stand.

In our slumber of comfort, we have allowed ourselves to be compromised. A widening polarization combined with the concession of American principles, our core beliefs, and national unity has led to the fade of our resistance to the form of governance that is eroding the fabric of our Republic. Out of desperation and the realization that we are, in effect, destroying ourselves, these pages are offered as a writ for action. A summons that can no longer be avoided.

Before proceeding to a group hug, we must first acknowledge that we all have been duped. We are being led by the nose by false gods acting benevolent and self-righteous. This self-proclaimed authority and ruling class are quick to override the rights of the individual, falsely labeling and demonizing any who disagree or challenge their agency. Tyrants all, I say.

I am not suggesting that we trivially sweep away our differences. We are, in fact, human and individualistic by design. I am saying that we should acknowledge this ideal: Americans should unite for a common humanity, good, and purpose. By looking to a higher power for the answers to what divides us, we can break the current cycle of tribalism and redeem what once bonded us together.

Perhaps the sentiments contained in the following pages are not yet sufficiently fashionable to procure them general favor; a long habit of not thinking a thing wrong, gives it a superficial appearance of being right, and raises at first a formidable outcry in defense of custom. But the tumult soon subsides. Time makes more converts than reason.[5]

Thomas Paine's words above eloquently define the fate of America in 1776. Eerily, they cascade to the present day in 2024. Originally published anonymously, *Common Sense* was distributed as a public pamphlet advocating independence from Great Britain to the people of the Thirteen Colonies. In the spirit of our Founding Fathers, I offer my analysis to advocate for a renewed independence from the form of government and the cultural divide that has overtaken and weakened the Republic. Some may call my words political rhetoric. I am not offering a political stance or position. Like Paine, this is a moral argument. See these words as a warning, no different than the canary in the coal mine, an indicator of impending danger. I am conveying the warning that our America and human freedoms as we know them are at stake. This warning should not come as a surprise; regrettably, though, it will be for many.

For some, I may be preaching to the choir; others may see this as a personal affront. Many will scoff. Sadly, my warning will be put down or ignored by millions of disenfranchised, uninformed Americans who have been intentionally distracted and/or diminished by their so-called moral leaders. Understandably, when our viewpoint is challenged, we become scared, defensive, and even vigorously opposed to altering perspectives. However, to find unity through revolution we must all be willing to open our minds and hearts.

No different than King George III in 1775, the modern-day political machine will look at my words as an insurrectionary theory and cry, "a threat to democracy!" When in fact they are an attempt to save the Republic. By writing this book, I am not advocating for violence. I simply ask that our backs become firmer and that we may stand steadfast against the headwinds of tyranny from within.

The reader is asked to reexamine Paine's words through the context of a present-day lens. Regrettably, many of our leaders today exhibit similar behaviors as referenced in the following excerpt:

> *But it is not so much the absurdity as the evil of hereditary succession which concerns mankind. Did it ensure a race of good and wise men it would have the seal of divine authority, but as it opens a door to the foolish, the wicked, and the improper, it hath in it the nature of oppression. Men who look upon themselves born to reign, and others to obey, soon grow insolent. Selected from the rest of mankind, their minds are early poisoned by importance; and the world they act in differs so materially from the world at large, that they have but little opportunity of knowing its true interests, and when they succeed to the government are frequently the most ignorant and unfit of any throughout the dominions.[6]*

Considering the current state and fate of one's homeland, do these words and the actions of our so-called leaders not sicken the sane man?

Paine wisely examined the state of affairs and concluded revolution was the only plausible solution. I now offer a similar verdict, although the brand of change for which I propose is benign in nature. Fear not as there are divine alternatives to the problems we face. Any other proclamation should be challenged because a Second Revolution, if misguided, will only stress society and the nation's fabric to its core. Similar to Paine in his 1776 pamphlet—who courageously railed against King George III, the monarchy, and hereditary succession, advocating independence from Great Britain to people in the Thirteen Colonies—I hope to offer a compelling petition to the citizens of this great nation.

Like Paine, I have chosen a pen to function as a sword in an effort to cut away at the tyranny that has consumed our once-great nation. In the pages that follow, I hope the reader will accept the position that a Second Revolution for our freedom is needed. In the best interest of America, the good citizens of this country can no longer relinquish their vote or their liberty to incompetent and corrupt governance. Please consider this editorial as a petition to the government for a redress of grievances.

Before the healing process can begin, we must all first endure the painful process of debridement. In this editorial, I will outline my perspective of America, her strengths and flaws, and propose a potential cure. My viewpoint will not be popular with all of my fellow Americans, yet I hope we can ultimately find common ground through common sense. In the spirit of Thomas Paine: "In the following pages I offer nothing more than simple facts, plain arguments, and common sense":[7] Through faith in a higher power, I put forth these visions and recommendations in hope for a better future and *For Love of Country.*

We the People

Rome has grown since its humble beginnings that it is now overwhelmed by its own greatness.

—TITUS LIVIUS (LIVY)

Some may argue that we are a late-stage republic destined to follow the footsteps of past empires only to become a historical footnote for posterity. I refuse to accept this diagnosis. Is our republic seriously ill and in need of immediate care? Absolutely. Are we terminally ill? I submit not. There is still treatment available to cure the disease of complacency that rots within. Similar to a patient with cancer, we must make the very difficult decision and choose a risky and disruptive treatment to prolong life and to reduce the destructive symptoms and the disease that plagues our republic.

The American republic started from humble beginnings. Founded on Judeo-Christian values and Greek laws, the United States of America is the culmination of many great societies and ideals. While an imperfect union, America is the greatest social experiment known to mankind. Its place in the world is still justified and needed. Our time is not over, and we owe it to the people of this nation and of the world to fight for life, liberty, and the pursuit of happiness.

Those who fought to correct the sins of their time also foretold potential future results and equipped us with the antidote to correct our ailment. Our forefathers understood the frailty of mankind. Knowing that all men are flawed by nature, and we would eventually poison our own well-being, they provided us with the solution to an inevitable outcome.

At current, *We the People* are lulled by fake priorities and are distracted by destructive fodder. Will we remain paralyzed by comfort, or can we break free from our paralysis and downward spiral? Overcome by false idols, our master's perceived greatness, and much complacency, we stand at the crossroads. We can follow the path of past empires only to fade away, or we can swallow the medicine needed to treat what ails us. Within our founding decree, a prescription was provided. *We the People* hold the key to our future. We can either exercise all options afforded to us by much greater and wiser men, or we can wither and die. I choose life, liberty, and the pursuit of happiness.

The Roman Empire lasted for well over half a millennium, from its formation until its demise. The United States of America has yet to reach its semi-quincentennial anniversary and half of the Roman Empire's existence. Surely with our potential, we can make a course correction from our current path. Certainly, America's destiny is not going to flame out without a fight. The premature cessation of this nation should be unacceptable to every patriot and citizen.

Look no further than the framework of the American republic. Three documents—the Declaration of Independence, the Constitution of the United States of America, and the Bill of Rights—established the construct of our great nation. Over time, our elected, appointed representatives have, in their perverted wisdom, overcomplicated the Founding Fathers' original intent to the point that an opposite desired effect has been implemented. What was originally engineered to provide jurisdictional guiderails "to create a government with enough power to act on a national level, but without so much power that fundamental rights would be at risk"[8] has been upended. Today, the preamble to most federal laws being brought forward consists of more words than the three founding documents combined. Frighteningly, it is without exaggeration that it is nearly impossible to tally the current number of federal laws in force.

What common sense exists if we cannot easily comprehend the laws of the land? I ask the reader to reflect upon the foundational framework of our land. Within these words (and with bolded passages by me for emphasis) is a hard pill that must be swallowed. For within is the cure for what ails our republic. Simply, these three foundational documents are all we need to guide us to a healthy recovery.

The Declaration of Independence

In Congress, July 4, 1776

The unanimous Declaration of the thirteen united States of America,

When in the Course of human events, it becomes necessary for one people to dissolve the political bands which have connected them with another, and to assume among the powers of the earth, the separate and equal station to which the Laws of Nature and of Nature's God entitle them, a decent respect to the opinions of mankind requires that they should declare the causes which impel them to the separation.

We hold these truths to be self-evident, that all men are created equal, that they are endowed by their Creator with certain unalienable Rights, that among these are Life, Liberty and the pursuit of Happiness. **—That to secure these rights, Governments are instituted among Men, deriving their just powers from the consent of the governed,—That whenever any Form of Government becomes destructive of these ends, it is the Right of the People to alter or to abolish it, and to institute new Government, laying its foundation on such principles and organizing its powers in such form, as to them shall seem most likely to effect their Safety and Happiness.** *Prudence, indeed, will dictate that Governments long established should not be changed for light and transient causes; and accordingly all experience hath shewn, that mankind are more disposed to suffer, while evils are sufferable, than to right themselves by abolishing the forms to which they are accustomed. But when a long train of abuses and usurpations, pursuing invariably the same*

Object evinces a design to reduce them under absolute Despotism, it is their right, it is their duty, to throw off such Government, and to provide new Guards for their future security.

The Constitution of the United States of America

We the People *of the United States, in Order to form a more perfect Union, establish Justice, insure domestic Tranquility, provide for the common defence, promote the general Welfare, and secure the Blessings of Liberty to ourselves and our Posterity, do ordain and establish this Constitution for the United States of America.*[9]

The Bill of Rights

Amendment I: *Congress shall make no law respecting an establishment of religion, or prohibiting the free exercise thereof; or abridging the freedom of speech, or of the press; or the right of the people peaceably to assemble, and to petition the Government for a redress of grievances.*

Amendment II: A well regulated Militia, being necessary to the security of a free State, the right of the people to keep and bear Arms, shall not be infringed.

Amendment III: No Soldier shall, in time of peace be quartered in any house, without the consent of the Owner, nor in time of war, but in a manner to be prescribed by law.

Amendment IV: The right of the people to be secure in their persons, houses, papers, and effects, against unreasonable searches and seizures, shall not be violated, and no Warrants shall issue, but upon probable cause, supported by Oath or affirmation, and particularly describing the place to be searched, and the persons or things to be seized.

Amendment V: No person shall be held to answer for a capital, or otherwise infamous crime, unless on a presentment or indictment of a Grand Jury, except in cases arising in the land or naval forces, or in the Militia, when in actual service in time of War or public danger; nor shall any person be subject for the same offence to be twice put in jeopardy of life or limb; nor shall be compelled in any criminal case to be a witness against himself, nor be deprived of life, liberty, or property, without due process of law; nor shall private property be taken for public use, without just compensation.

Amendment VI: In all criminal prosecutions, the accused shall enjoy the right to a speedy and public trial, by an impartial jury of the State and district wherein the crime shall have been committed, which district shall have been previously ascertained by law, and to be informed of the nature and cause of the accusation; to be confronted with the witnesses against him; to have compulsory process for obtaining witnesses in his favor, and to have the Assistance of Counsel for his defense.

Amendment VII: In suits at common law, where the value in controversy shall exceed twenty dollars, the right of trial by jury shall be preserved, and no fact tried by a jury, shall be otherwise re-examined in any Court of the United States, than according to the rules of the common law.

Amendment VIII: Excessive bail shall not be required, nor excessive fines imposed, nor cruel and unusual punishments inflicted.

Amendment IX: The enumeration in the Constitution, of certain rights, shall not be construed to deny or disparage others retained by the people.

Amendment X: The powers not delegated to the United States by the Constitution, nor prohibited by it to the States, are reserved to the States respectively, or to the people.[10]

Humbly, the basic rights established upon our founding are sacrosanct and should have never been perverted. While old-fashioned, willingly straying from these basic principles has facilitated the deterioration of our republic. As a result, our current system of government has far exceeded the boundaries set forth within the founding provisions. It is time that we return to our roots. A rejuvenation and simplification of our current system is necessary to restore natural order. The desired nobler government can only bloom from the less complex and orderly framework. Montesquieu once quipped: "The deterioration of every government begins with the decay of the principle upon which it was founded."[11] I declare it is now time to return America to the principles upon which she was founded.

As written in the unanimous Declaration, "it is the Right of the People to alter or to abolish it, and to institute new Government." The time has come for the good people of this nation to rise up, enact, and engage in a Second Revolution. While not all will agree with the author's forthcoming positions or the prescribed means for saving our nation, disagreement on a proposed method is expected and warranted. What is not up for discussion is the need and urgency for this intervention. We must protect and safeguard our republic.

A Threat
to Democracy

> *If we do not make common cause to save the good old ship of the Union on this voyage, nobody will have a chance to pilot her on another voyage.*
>
> —ABRAHAM LINCOLN

Some may espouse that I am an unabashed "threat to democracy!" This label is one that I can comfortably live with. Being a threat to the modern-day democracy is a must for all patriots. More than just wordplay, a democracy is contrary to our constitutional republic and is an illegitimate form of government. The uninformed believe that *democracy* and *republic* are synonymous, yet they deliver very different results. Some of our leaders even deliberately use the word *democracy* when describing our nation, and in doing so seek to alter the truth.

Within a pure democracy, power is held by the population as a whole; whereas within a republic, power is held by individual citizens. When it comes to making laws, in a democracy, a voting majority has almost unlimited power, but minorities have few protections from the will of the majority; whereas in a republic, the people elect representatives to make laws according to the constraints of a constitution. Similarly, in a democracy, people are ruled by the majority; whereas in a republic, laws are made by elected representatives of the people. Finally, when it comes to the protection of rights, in a democracy, rights can be overridden by the will of the majority; whereas in a republic, a constitution protects the rights of all people from the will of the majority. The United States of America is a constitutional republic and *not* a democracy. Thus, in America, sovereignty should rest with the people.

Government is the work of man's hands. Even the original forming of our government was the creation of men, yet natural law was considered. Our forefathers wanted *We the People* to be free from tyranny. That is why they risked all to form a constitutional republic. If they had felt a democracy was the better path, that it would maintain natural law and individual liberties, then they would have established a democracy. But they did not. A democracy is one step closer to communism where the "State" (i.e., the proletariat ruling class) and the majority rules. Currently, "the majority" leading our country is now led by a tyrant-minority. As such, the so-called majority ends up being a small group of people with all the power, authority, and wealth that they can accumulate. Contrary to what the Founding Fathers wanted, a democracy has nothing to do with what is best for the individual. Our Founders wanted us to have those rights that were ordained to us by our Creator. God did not create government. God created man, and man created government as a tool to manage itself. Unfortunately, this tool has now become weaponized against its Maker. Our current government no longer serves the people; it serves itself and its masters. Out of control, it does its own bidding and no longer serves the interests of the people for whom it was created.

It has come to the point in our country's history that only special interest groups have the majority. No longer will it be the masses or *We the People* who rule our land. It certainly won't be the forgotten or marginalized who will be protected. It will be those who are marginalizing others that will retain all the power. Aristotle provided fair warning when he succinctly outlined the future state of a republic: "Republics decline into democracies and democracies degenerate into despotisms."[12] It seems America is sliding into the second phase of this prophecy, which is why a Second Revolution is in order.

Over four decades ago during his inaugural address on January 20, 1981, President Reagan identified the very problem that we now face:

> *In this present crisis, government is not the solution to our problem; government is the problem. From time to time we've been tempted to believe that society has become too complex to be managed by self-rule, that government by an elite group is superior to government for, by, and of the people. Well, if no one among us is capable of governing himself, then who among us has the capacity to govern someone else? All of us together, in and out of government, must bear the burden. The solutions we seek must be equitable, with no one group singled out to pay a higher price.*
>
> *We hear much of special interest groups. Well, our concern must be for a special interest group that has been too long neglected. It knows no sectional boundaries or ethnic and racial*

divisions, and it crosses political party lines. It is made up of men and women who raise our food, patrol our streets, man our mines and factories, teach our children, keep our homes, and heal us when we're sick—professionals, industrialists, shopkeepers, clerks, cabbies, and truckdrivers. They are, in short, 'We the people,' this breed called Americans.

So, as we begin, let us take inventory. We are a nation that has a government—not the other way around. And this makes us special among the nations of the Earth. Our government has no power except that granted it by the people. It is time to check and reverse the growth of government, which shows signs of having grown beyond the consent of the governed.

Regrettably, the good works put forth many decades ago have been eroded by the threat from our current democracy. The bulwark of our constitutional republic must be strengthened against the rising tide of tyranny.

I'm not suggesting that we alter the framework of our current republic. Rather, I am suggesting that we return to its founding principles and intended structure of government. In this Second Revolution for freedom, I am asking the

American people to stand up and recognize that their rights are being infringed upon, demand that our representative government work within the framework of our Constitution, and be opposed to a feel-good totalitarian democracy, which is being levied against American citizens.

The Threat
Among Us

Common sense will tell us, that the power
which hath endeavored to subdue us,
is of all others, the most improper to defend.

—THOMAS PAINE

There are countless enemies in this world who despise America and wish her harm; regrettably, many exist within her borders. The self-proclaimed disenfranchised can hate America and have the right to speak ill about her, yet they do not have the right to tread on the freedom of others or circumvent constitutional rights endowed by law.

This authoritarian scourge has infiltrated our republic by altering our language, modifying our history, or stripping our culture of the elements that originally united us. The traditional family unit, community, cultural rituals, organized religion, and even the act of hard work have all been marginalized. The intentional degradation of American society and cultural values has been a decades-long vendetta perpetrated by those who wish to rule her. Her ideals have been cast aside like the plastic Chinese garbage that pollutes our daily existence and litters our local landfills.

It is not my intent to spread doomsday fears or gin up conspiracy theories; rather, I wish to raise my concern about the current direction of our nation. It is disheartening to witness the evolution of who we are becoming as people. For some, "Everything is great!" However, and regrettably, for those of us who take for granted the gift that we have been bestowed, many will eventually and without concern march like lambs to the slaughter. I do not intend to be one of them.

Over the past decade, our country has experienced a rapid decline in traditional American values, beliefs, customs, and culture. To alter this course, we must remove our blinders, examine our current state of being, set aside our differences, and strive to do better. The threat among us has saturated the American psyche and all elements of day-to-day life, thus making most complacent to their existence and some even complicit in their dissemination. Ultimately, there has to be a shared understanding of the current state of affairs before we can collectively agree to overcome any of these items. The following categories are not all-encompassing and, when examined individually, do not raise concerns for most Americans. Yet when combined, they should send alarm bells off for all.

American Values and Culture

In recent years, we have witnessed a decay of our values and cultural norms perpetrated by power-hungry tyrants who care more about their own self-importance than the well-being of their neighbor. We have strayed from our mooring, and our moral compass is malfunctioning, as if the needle has been physically restrained by a counterintuitive magnetic field.

As a nation, we struggle to maintain our heritage and basic principles. The self-proclaimed overlords of society have worked diligently to subvert traditional American values down to the wholesale perversion of our language, all purposely orchestrated in an effort to manipulate the masses. We are bombarded daily by nonsensical contemporary cultural norms and distracted by woke ideology, propagated rage, cancel culture, and anti-American sentiment. We are being intentionally driven to a lack of respect and empathy for our fellow citizens. We have been forced to abandon our virtues, blessings, and patriotism all in the name of Critical Race Theory (CRT), White privilege, and gender misappropriation, which are dictated by the tyrant-minority. Like it or not, partisans on both sides of the aisle are responsible for the erosion of societal values and social norms.

Too many have become chronic victims, apoplectic over conflicting viewpoints. We need to bring an end to the increasing insanity affecting our culture. A never-ending stream of negativity feeds into the general population's discontent, only nurturing our narcissistic beliefs. Does the American public really believe that our adversaries are wasting time teaching their children the virtues of gender study, CRT, or discussing the benefits of life-altering transgender reconstructive surgery?

I do not wish to diminish the American people; we all have our differences and faults. However, I cannot idly stand by and watch as good Americans live in disorder and decay, forfeiting their rights in order to socially "feel good" while they virtue signal about nonsensical issues.

Free Speech

I appeal to the reader's good senses; let my words be a weathervane for tolerance and acceptance. It will not come as a surprise if my remarks are labeled divisive, untrue, or censored—even though much of what is written is based on historical facts. There was a time in history when opposing viewpoints could be debated vigorously and still result in an agreeable solution; today, however, words we disagree with are labeled as violence. While my views may be unpopular for some, it is a civic duty (responsibility) to communicate what many are thinking. Words may be disruptive for some of the fainthearted, yet words alone do not equate to violence. Free and unencumbered speech, spoken or written truths are the light that disinfects.

For those victims in our society who feel threatened by mere words, look no further than the First Amendment: "Congress shall make no law respecting an establishment of religion, or prohibiting the free exercise thereof; or abridging the freedom of speech, or of the press; or the right of the people peaceably to assemble, and to petition the Government for a redress of grievances." After a deep, cleansing breath, simply bask in the knowledge of the law that protects your ability to challenge the words of your opponent also protects the words that you object. However, please retain the following truth: feeling offended is not protected by the Constitution.

History

Why are so many bent on rewriting history? We cannot change the past or apply modern-day standards and sensibilities to events of a bygone era. Any attempts to do so or to make excuses for people we never personally knew are simply an exercise in tolerance. At a minimum, we should try to forgive, accept it, learn from it, and make efforts not to repeat the same mistakes. Those living in the past or bent on rewriting it are only doing so to gin up division.

George Santayana wisely stated, "Those who do not remember the past are condemned to repeat it."[13] By examining history, I am not suggesting that we live in the past. However, we should not attempt to reshape our history. It is unhealthy for her citizens when history is allowed to be rewritten to suit certain modern benefits or immoral individuals who wish to change the narrative.

Take the recent movement to tear down historical monuments. While I acknowledge that the subjects of these memorials were offensive to most, what benefits come from destroying history? What's next? Are we going to tear down paintings from museum walls? Are we going to burn books on subject matters that some people don't agree with? Are we going to pave roadways with the headstones of our supposed enemies whom we cannot come to terms with? I would argue that the fascists among us are the people who are tearing down our history in the name of social justice without the respect of the bloodshed that occurred to warrant such memorials.

Please do not mistake my words. I denounce all forms of evil and hate that exist in the world, both in our past and current. There should be no place for it. However, any attempts to erase the past, no matter how vile, only condemns us to repeat it. Good can come from bad events if we take the time to educate ourselves. I also do not believe that all of America's interventions within the world were morally right or justifiable. America is not without her flaws, yet all skeletons of the past are those created by man.

Equality vs. Equity

Nowhere else in the world is there such a diverse makeup of its population that exists within America. Our diversity makes us unique and stronger, and it most certainly should not be used to divide us. One's gender, race, ethnicity, religious belief, sexual orientation, or political affiliation should not matter; as Americans, we should only be measured on the content of our character, our good works, and our merits. Ultimately, the good that we bring to the world and the love that we express to each other should earn higher marks than the pigment of our skin.

By employing equity, some in society are attempting to socially engineer or correct those traits that none of us have control over. Equality is the only unit of measure that benefits society; anything less is intended to divide us.

Unity

In recent years we have become a very polarized and divided country. Through our complacency and narcissism, we have allowed socially engineered constructs to lead us down a treacherous and thorny path of national disunity. Instead of uniting us, we are intentionally being subdivided into tribes.

While no one who remembers wants to see tragedy unfold, the last time our republic was truly united was on Wednesday, September 12, 2001, when fear of the unknown transitioned to anger. This white-hot wrath stemming from the prior day's attack sparked a national allegiance not experienced for more than a half century. Will it require another act of aggression against America before its people find commonality? One could argue that we are currently under attack from within.

Our forefathers knew our long-term success would be tied to a united front. In 1776, John Adams, Benjamin Franklin, and Thomas Jefferson proposed the motto for the first Great Seal of the United States, "*E Pluribus Unum.*" This Latin phrase, which means "one from many," signified a strong statement of the American determination to form a single nation from a collection of states. I would submit to the reader that, like our forefathers, we should seek unity while respecting the diversity of our many people. Our differing backgrounds and beliefs should only enhance the melting pot of this once-great social experiment.

In his last public speech in 1799, Patrick Henry proclaimed, "Let us trust God, and our better judgment to set us right hereafter. United we stand, divided we fall." This reminds us that those forces who aim to divide us do so with ill intent. We must root out the seeds of racial discontent, claims of inequity, and other fabricated wedges sown by our nation's dissenters.

While we allow our narcissistic behavior to overwhelm us and be distracted by superfluous nonsense, nations like China are running out in front of us. Our true enemies are preparing to replace us, as we are not standing together as *We the People* or as a united nation.

Our ability to rally in the past saved the world on more than one occasion. America's strength lies within its united citizens. It is incumbent upon us as citizens to remember our history and not allow the current prevailing force to topple us. I am not advocating for violence or sanctioning unruliness. I am simply stating that we must revisit our roots and who we are as a nation. Look back at our ancestry without malice, understand that we are imperfect, and acknowledge that we cannot apply today's cultural values and norms to historical events that occurred over the past two centuries.

Religion

The enemies of America have been chipping away at her foundation for decades. In the face of an era of "go along to get along," the masses allowed a tyrant-minority to bully society into removing God from our day-to-day lives. No more would "one nation under God" be recited in our classrooms. The removal of God and other forms of faith-based teachings from our schools was intentional. Further, organized religions are being attacked and harassed by elements of the ruling class as faith unites the populist. There is no room for God in the communist world. There can only be one supreme power, and that is the communist "state," the ruling class.[14]

While I fully support the separation of church and state, an appeal to the readers' emotions ought to remind oneself that the only amount of virtue signaling that should occur in society is acknowledging the importance of faith in our lives, our families, and our communities.

Law, Order, and Truth

We are a nation of laws. Most are happy to abide by the law and live within the construct of our society, while some are allowed to roam unabashed like a pack of hyenas. A world without laws is anarchy. Today, America has evolved into two sets of laws: one for those in power and another for those being ruled. Laws are meant to protect civil society.

Recently, a moral sickness within society has been propagated; fringe political groups under the guise of "anti-fascist" are intentionally used as a tool to harass and intimidate. These instruments are paraded out in order to deter good people from rejecting anarchists or the decisions of the ruling class. A movement in which the belief is that differing viewpoints are a personal affront, which equates to violence and should be met with reciprocal violence. Both sides of the political spectrum have their fringe elements. However, it is not a stretch to believe that most do not wish to reside in turmoil and will happily live in harmony even if we do not always agree.

In an effort to further divide us and advance an anti-American ideology, a coordinated effort to propagate, rebrand, or repackage the truth has fully blossomed. The nonstop distribution of coordinated misinformation is transmitted on so many channels and at such a velocity that the consumer has little hope of separating the wheat (truth) from the chaff. Through our complacency, we do not pause long enough to recognize that the repeated transmission of a known falsehood or untruth does not change a lie into the truth. Also, changing language to suit one's narrative does not make a lie the truth. A lie is still a lie. Several tyrants have openly proclaimed, "He who controls the language rules the world."[15] The American populous should be more vigilant and verify what they are digesting.

Media and Technology

The advent of the 24/7 news cycle, social media, biased algorithms, and artificial intelligence have only expedited the polarization process and aided the ruling class. State-coordinated propaganda media of all biases is the primary podium for the distribution of tribalism and fear. While all outlets are protected by the First Amendment, we are not obliged to consume their spin. At a minimum, understand there is a synchronized agenda behind most everything that you ingest.

In a short time, the age of technology has grown like kudzu, invading all facets of our existence. I would submit to the reader that recent developments in technology offer some societal benefits, and yes, they have brought amazing developments to mankind. However, like the creeping "mile-a-minute" vine, if left unchecked, this quiet killer will overtake and grow over everything in its path util it eventually finds its way into every corner of our daily lives.

I implore the good citizens of this nation to look beyond the length of their arms and the tiny screen in their hands to recognize that a better future is fading away in the distance. While technology has indeed brought efficiency to our world, it has also opened the door to malaise. Unfortunately, most will not hear my message or heed my warnings, as they are not being served up in thirty-second TikTok snippets.

Society has become enamored by the pings of notifications that send our brain into overdrive. The nonstop dopamine hits shield us from the reality that technology has a very dark side. There is a reason why the inventors of this technology do not allow their own children to use it or have limited usage. The all-seeing telescreens and watchful eye are no substitute for face-to-face communication.

Beyond connecting us, the advent of social media has emotionally crippled a generation of young people. Praying upon their insecurities, it has stripped society of its many core values. While we willingly use our devices to distract or occupy time, it threatens and preys upon our youth.

In addition to becoming every person's leash, big tech has further suppressed free speech either through digital blacklists, biased algorithms, shadow banning, or blatant censorship. Individual freedom, our right to express thoughts and free speech, is sacrosanct. This right should not be stifled by any entity. Yet we panic at the thought of losing our devices.

The reader should be reminded that a singular belief dominance in the tech world, or legacy media, does not benefit anyone in our nation except the so-called ruling class. As well, it should not be a surprise that some within our population would openly give up their freedom in exchange for an app that comes with the promise that it will solve the problems that ail our republic.

Liberty and Freedom

Liberty, rugged individualism, ingenuity, and commerce are the qualities that built America more than once yet are now being avoided in favor of cheap Chinese manufacturing, a Green New Deal, and gender dysphoria. The principles that we were founded upon must be brought to the forefront of our daily lives through open, intelligent, intentional, and courteous debate. *We the People* must act. If ignored, the poisonous cancer of communism will metastasize to the point that American values and beliefs become a distant memory.

We are all busy living our daily lives. However, this excuse becomes a form of complacency as we allow mediocrity to flourish. When will the American people say they've had enough and stand for logic and reason? If we do not reign in the efforts to polarize us, we are, by default, freely handing away our liberties and freedom.

Now adrift, America's sails are torn, and her rudder is damaged. Our future is at stake if we do not return to port, back to our roots and American values. To do so takes action. Pay heed. You can no longer stand idly by—you must act. Remember, silence equates to acceptance. By saying or doing nothing, you are accepting the chaos that is being thrust upon us all. Do not allow a loud minority viewpoint to deter you from action. Let your voice be heard. Let it ring for truth, liberty, and freedom. Stand up for what you believe in.

In order to save our nation, we have to reverse Marxist cultural trends that are eroding the sanctity of our society.[16] In lieu of shunning patriotism or allowing anti-Americanism to occur, we should embrace our heritage. Embrace patriotism. Embrace our traditions, institutions, and ideals. Embrace the family unit and raise thoughtful and morally grounded children. Embrace religion and community. Embrace each other as united citizens. Celebrate those things that make us strong, admired, and sought after. I would argue that "The tree of liberty"[17] needs to be nourished not with the blood of its countrymen, but with the rejuvenating waters of patriotism. A rebinding of traditional American values, beliefs, and behaviors. Without action, there are only hollow words and empty truths. Common sense and our history should dictate that Americans will stand for liberty and freedom. Will you protect these natural laws granted to all? Will you stand for a Second Revolution, a moral revolution?

Sovereignty
Matters

But I fear, that in every assembly, Members
will obtain an Influence, by Noise not sense.
By Meanness, not Greatness. By Ignorance not
Learning. By contracted Hearts not large souls . . .
There must be decency and respect. . . .

—JOHN ADAMS

As things stand today, there is a two-pronged assault on the soul of the American people and the world. A struggle of good against evil. Through these attacks, self-appointed global elites seek to cripple our national and individual sovereignty. Thus, the greatest existential threat to the world is not global warming but rather the ultimate loss of liberty and freedom for its citizens.

The first prong of this assault is lesser known to many, which makes it more threatening, as it is allowed to freely permeate into the governments of the West. America's (and other

Western countries') national sovereignty is being fragmented from the inside out. In a nutshell, our national sovereignty has been abdicated to the highest bidder, foreign combatants, and the power-hungry ruling class who believe they have the right cure for what ails us.

Look no further than the Swiss Alps for this root of evil. The world does not require another German megalomaniac overlord preaching from the mountains about a fourth Industrial Revolution, a great reset, or any other systemic restructuring required for the "benefit" of all. I ask that someone please explain to me: Who nominated the Davos elites to speak and act on our behalf? What credentials do these self-appointed "trustees" hold that gives them ultimate power and authority over our country and the world?

The last time a singular governing party attempted to rule the world was during World War II, when the world lost more than sixty million people. No one ruling class should be above the individual rights of the people. However, hidden behind the veil of altruism, this self-absorbed group plotted their subversive dismantling of individual liberty all in the name of moral superiority. In this age of globalization, foreign actors, and orchestrated international events, one does not have to look far to find ill intent and hypocrisy. No one entity shall supersede or infringe upon individual rights of Americans, yet under the guise of public/private cooperation, this is exactly their intent through public shaming by imposing carbon footprint guilt or other guilt-provoking means on its global citizens.

America's dissenters are employing an apoc-alyptic green agenda comprised of environmental, social, and governance (ESG) scores all in an effort to measure a human's worth. In addition to their intended mastery of the digital world and all that it controls, there is an absolute allegiance to this cult agenda, which many willing citizens are blindly consuming as if it were the order of the day. While their proposed solutions are carefully crafted to appear harmless, America's citizens should not stand for unelected global elitists espousing how government should hold absolute control over individual rights, privileges, and our free will. So be warned and be wary of any proposed form of global governance. And do not be charmed by their trinkets and faux altruistic offerings disguised as globally backed digital currencies or other forms of well-meaning benefits.

Dear Americans and global citizens, please understand that you are being fed poison on a daily basis by globalists seeking your money and power. Please understand that if you don't ultimately measure up, you will be asked to drink the Kool-Aid.[18] Do not allow the forked tongues of serpents to persuade you otherwise. Recognize, then reject, their venomous lies cascaded and shrouded in fearmongering speech. Please stand up for your rights and refuse to subscribe to their global agenda. Reject the hubris of self-proclaimed titans of human civilization, individuals who feel they have the right to reengineer the species and the human spirit.

The second prong is a true inside job—clearly being orchestrated by those who should have our best interests at heart and the laws of the land and our Constitution before anything else. There are too many events occurring on a daily basis to even begin to try to unpack the transgressions by our government and from outside foreign actors against the American people. (If the reader wishes to educate themself, there are numerous examples highlighted publicly. To find the truth, it would be recommended that you look beyond your chosen narrative provided to you by an external algorithm.)

While it won't surprise the well-informed, it may shock others that the American people are being ideologically manipulated both at home and abroad. The exploitation of America's goodwill has manifested itself into a loss of faith in American institutions from mainstream media to social media and, more notably, the government. What was first established with the sole purpose to serve the best interests, protect the sovereignty of the American people, and—more importantly—to uphold the Constitution of the United States, the federal government has exploded into a swamp of more than 440 separate agencies, many of which have elements that are counter to the American people.

A progressive agenda and hyper-politics have sidelined our individual sovereignty and one's ability to self-govern in exchange for the worst form of government: a bureaucratic state of aristocracy sold to us as a benevolent democracy. One generation away from totalitarianism, any form of self-governance, freedom, and individual liberty could soon be stripped from the American people. Like it or not, the recent pandemic was a dry run of ultimate government control and overreach. Thomas Paine warns, "A body of men holding themselves accountable to nobody ought not to be trusted by anybody." Have any of our recent leaders been held accountable for their transgressions against the American people or the United States Constitution during the recent shutdown years? I submit not. Sadly, the American people continually hand the keys of oppression back to their jailers while the same corrupt jailers hold supreme power over the body politic.

A compromised government cannot and will not investigate itself. Only patriot whistleblowers, incorruptible newcomers within the government, real investigative journalists, and/or other hardened Americans embodied with a steel will and without fear of reprisal can truly shed the antiseptic light upon the disease that plagues our sick government.

Individual sovereignty should equate to freedom from external control, self-governance, and autonomy. Many years prior to the publication of Thomas Paine's *Common Sense*, John Locke anonymously published an essay with themes that strongly influenced the writers of our Constitution.[19] Locke was a firm believer in natural rights. Simply stated, our rights of "life, liberty and property" are God-given and can never be taken or given away. These rights place sovereignty in the hands of the people. Locke also strongly felt that "the people shall be judge; for who shall be judge whether his trustee or deputy acts well and according to the trust reposed in him, but he who deputes him and must, by having deputed him, have still a power to discard him when he fails in his trust?"

Locke, like our later Declaration of Independence, correctly states that *We the People* have the power, right, and obligation to hold our representatives to account for their misuse of our trust. In this, the Second Revolution, we the American people, to protect our republic, must enact controlling influence over our representative government and their power, if necessary, to overthrow said representatives who knowingly abused the rights and the trust of the American people. I do not espouse violence; instead, I support voting out representatives who don't act as representatives of their constituents. We must eradicate the bad actors and poor representatives from our government offices and agencies.

The reader should remember that in America, any form of governance other than a constitutional republic is illegitimate and lacks the right to coerce people to obey it. It lacks the right to subvert our sovereignty. All attempts to gain dominion over *We the People* should be forcefully rebuffed. In a Second Revolution, aren't free people called upon, if not obligated, to rise up, stand resolute, and claim their independence? Any lesser action relinquishes one's ability to self-govern.

Taxation Without Representation

---

*For decades, we have piled deficit upon deficit,
mortgaging our future and our children's future
for the temporary convenience of the present.*

—RONALD REGAN

In 1765, the Crown and British Parliament
approved the Stamp Act, requiring colonists
to pay taxes on every page of printed paper
they used and included fees on playing cards and
dice. The proceeds from this tax were intended to
defray the expenses associated with British troops
(who settled on the continent) for their protection
and defense of the Colonies from attack. Unable to
elect representatives in Parliament, the colonists
felt their natural rights were being trampled upon.
Thus, the rallying cry and political movement
of "No taxation without representation!"[20] was
adopted. This new sales tax would ultimately
lead to protests and revolution by the colonists. I

would submit that the rights of future generations of Americans are being violated by a similar act of taxation.

By the end of 2001, the U.S. national debt equaled $5.81 trillion,[21] which equated to a 55 percent debt-to-GDP ratio. By December 2023, it has ballooned north of $33.96 trillion with a 122 percent debt-to-GDP ratio. This translates to a personal debt of $93,655 for every person living in America. By the time of this publishing, the U.S. national debt will exceed $34.0 trillion, an unsustainable figure that looms over every man, woman, and child.

In rough numbers, if the median family annual income in the United States were $75,000 and that same family spent money like our federal government, it would spend $125,000 per year. Which means that a single-family would have to put $50,000 on a credit card during that same year, despite already being $500,000 in debt. It is insane to believe that any one of us would be allowed to act so irresponsibly. What credit card company or bank would float each of us $50,000 per year with no questions asked or without a plan to repay the debt? The normal person would be cut off and have their possessions repossessed, but our government continues to spend our money without limits.

Ideally, debt should be avoided. However, as a rule, no more than 36 percent of income should go toward total debt payments, including housing. The U.S. government's debt is approaching 123 percent of income. Like it or not, our government's reckless spending is a tax on all of us, and future generations will be stuck with this bill and all the associated late fees. An argument can be made that this is an absolute form of taxation without representation.

The Stamp Act of 1765 cost a colonist two-shilling six-pence for the purchase of a stamp (in today's dollars, this equates roughly to $13.00). This was equivalent to the cost of one day's wages for a skilled tradesman. At the time, this was obviously enough of a tax to foment a revolution. Today, in contrast, if we were required to pay off the national debt in full, the average American—every man, woman, and child—would have to pay more than a year's wages to offset the national debt. Have we simply lost sight of the value of a hard day's work? And why are we not enraged like the early colonists were over this blatant act of tyranny? The colonists risked much more for much less. Are we not willing to do the same?

I would ask the reader this: Has your standard of living improved over the last three-plus years? Or has it degraded, like your homeland? With the recent U.S. credit ratings downgrade, erosion of governance, and rising out-of-control deficits, America is effectively bankrupt. It seems that "Bidenomics" is working; the working class makes less and gets taxed while the corrupt get richer. I'm sorry to break the news to my fellow citizens that there is nothing free when it comes to our government. Government handouts always come with a price tag, if not payable via the IRS or through the forfeiture of our personal assets and/or our rights. Is this not enough reason to fight for our way of life? Is a second uprising not required to correct the blatant mismanagement of our financial well-being? Didn't our ancestors stand for much more over a lessor infraction?

Don't Tread on Me

Live free or die.
Death is not the greatest of evils.

—GENERAL JOHN STARK

The yellow Gadsden flag features a fierce coiled rattlesnake, a clear warning to Britain not to violate the liberties of the American subjects. With the text, "DONT TREAD ON ME" written in capitalized letters across the bottom, it is one of the most popular symbols of the American Revolution, an assertive warning of vigilance and willingness to act in defense against coercion.

Adopted in 1775, the Gadsden flag was originally created for the colonies fledgling navy and was painted on the drums of Continental Marines preparing for battle with the British. What once illustrated as a colonial united front displayed as a threat to the King's loyal subjects is now being divided up from within by corrupt agents. Sadly, this once-great symbol of freedom has somehow been perverted and is now considered by the uninformed as racist, an idea this patriot rejects.

While the "coiled snake" of the flag expanded from the original Thirteen Colonies to encompass all fifty states, its significance still represents American grit. Regrettably, however, the government powers that be have decided (for their own benefit) it is better for us to be the divided states of America—divided and dumbed down through the spread of fear, despair, and misinformation. In contrast, true patriots would aspire to lift us up, rally us together, and shine a light on our blessings. Thankful for the many opportunities, we should be a grateful nation and a thankful people for the blessing bestowed upon us by our Creator.

Regretfully, many do not understand what is being done to us, and the foundations that support our republic are intentionally being undermined. Our natural-born liberties are under attack and are eroding in front of our own eyes. Day by day, our freedom has been chipped away by nefarious actors and out-of-touch elites with socialistic beliefs. Relying upon a uniformed or complacent populous, these bad actors have downgraded and weaponized what was intended to be a representative government formed under the umbrella of a constitutional republic into a *banana republic*.[22] Through our complacency, we have abdicated our freedom to absolute government, like the jailed handing over the keys to their devilish jailers.

A representative government should do what is in the best interest of those being represented, with the caveat that they are in touch with the actual sensibilities, struggles, and necessities of those they govern. Instead, we are fed daily with veiled debilitating offerings or false charities disguised as a hand up that are only intended to keep the American populace docile, numb, and ignorant. I don't blame the American people (or other citizens around the globe) for their disengagement. Most simply want to live their lives in peace and don't want to wade into the quagmire of bovine excrement that is being piled neck deep around us on a daily basis. However, the malaise that shrouds us must be lifted before it is too late.

A large portion of the nation is being discounted. It appears that the powerful self-described elites are trying to revert America's citizens to their prescribed stations in life, no different than the serfs who were bound by the feudal system of work on his lord's estate. The

Turks had a homely proverb that they applied on such occasions. They said, "The fish stinks first at the head,"[23] meaning that if the servant is disorderly, it is because the master is so. *We the People* have become so disorderly that our actions, or lack of discipline, have opened the door to a subservient discontent, which has allowed a new breed of tyranny.

No longer hiding in the shadows, the nefarious actors endorsing this change have become fully brazen in their actions. Look no further than the recent two-year infringement of our rights, lockdowns, and an unprecedented shutdown of our economy during the COVID-19 pandemic. The simple freedom of movement, freedom of speech, and freedom of choice were stripped away without even a whimper. Constant misinformation and fearmongering cajoled a docile public into masking their faces and voices. The atrocities and betrayals against the American (and the world's) people should never be forgotten. Recently, these same actors are confident enough in their standing that they now tout that *We the People* acted freely during the COVID-19 pandemic. They say we volunteered and chose to subrogate our freedoms willingly as they had no authority or power to dictate our behaviors.

In 1887, Lord Acton (John Dalberg-Acton) profoundly stated, "Power tends to corrupt and absolute power corrupts absolutely. Great men are almost always bad men, even when they exercise influence and not authority; still more when you superadd the tendency of the certainty of corruption by authority."[24] Those in power expect and rely upon our complacency. This is evidenced by the career politicians who preach to their constituents out of one side of their mouth and cast their votes out of the other. With only the exception of a minority few, bribery, corruption, and the erosion of morality are the order of the day in our government.

Some may blame capitalism for this decline. However, our decline is due to those in power taking advantage (i.e., enriching themselves with power and wealth), and the citizenry allows it to occur through our complacency. In reality, our decline is hooked to the un-American religious zealots, false profits, and communist pundits from within who are the threat to our so-called democracy.

A number of Americans are waking to the truth. They are finally recognizing that communism, socialism, Marxism, fascism, and/or any other flavor of authoritarianism that now plagues our culture and poisons the waters of personal liberty with the sole purpose of self-gratification, power, and ultimate control is the root of decline within our society.

Communism (or socialism) is sold as a utopia, where the workingman finally gets his fair share, and the bourgeoisie gets their comeuppance, social just rewards. The workingman then hands over all control to the "state." This social justice theory fails to define what and who is the "state" other than "the proletariat organized as the ruling class." The naïve democratic socialist fails to recognize that all which is controlled by the "state" is still governed by authoritarian rulers. A small group with supreme powers over property, production, agriculture, and freedoms.

As prescribed in the communist handbook, the charter for the downtrodden workingman is to overthrow the current regime.[25] What is also defined within the manifesto is the clear abolishment of eternal truths, such as freedom and justice. This political theory clearly states that it will abolish "all religion and all morality," and it will centralize "the means of communication and transport in the hands of the State."[26] This antireligious cult offers nothing more than a fleeting dream of salvation and the destruction of personal liberty. Yet if nothing, it is true to its word. Look around you; these theories are being played out in our daily existence.

Sadly, look no further than George Orwell's two dystopian tales, *Animal Farm* and *Nineteen Eighty-Four*.[27] [28] Both works were published more than seven decades ago and written to warn of the dangers of democratic socialism and totalitarian systems, respectively. These nightmarish fables have been quietly playing out over the past decades within the United States without the majority of the population being any wiser or showing any signs of concerns. Yes, you read it correctly: a socialistic experiment has been unleashed on the American people, and most are oblivious; some are even complicit. This cancerous disease has crept through the majority of our governmental agencies. Some have sounded the warning, yet these cautionary flags go unnoticed by the masses or are labeled as misinformation.

Alas, the uninformed socialist might claim that socialism just hasn't been implemented right or enough for it to work properly. People who actually believe this nonsense have missed the opportunity to learn from the failed history of socialism. For if they had, they would have learned that socialism has been attempted many times and has failed on every occasion. A naïve socialist would say that we would be better off with equal distribution for all (equity), yet they fail to recognize that those in power still make the rules, and they will not be any more generous with their handouts. Not uncoincidentally, the federal government's steady diet of handouts is bankrupting our country, effectively enslaving all future generations.

One may find it ironic that the philosopher Karl Marx, who produced the revolutionary writings favoring socialism and a communist revolution, is the same theorist who stated, "History repeats itself, first as tragedy, then as farce." But yet there are some social elites who are desperately pushing America toward Marxism. Allowing this once-great nation to be brought to the edge of the communist cliffside is a travesty.

The reality is we have a communist cult issue, an alternative state of mind, and a false God named *government* that is being forced upon us all. One does not need to look very far to see its roots. The Washington uniparty has overstretched its authority like a rogue virus, invading every surface of our existence. The culmination of decades-long moral erosion, immersion in fear-filled propaganda, and the expansion of government control has withered the nation's willpower to withstand the bombardment from within. As advertised, these actions fundamentally changed our once-great nation—and not for the best. Any progress that was once made to bring us closer has been overridden by race-baiting communists, cancel culture, and woke ideology.

Some reading this may have a foundational antipathy toward my words. For the reader who emulates a visceral response to these words, triggering an automatic hatred and wanted demonization of the author or foments a desired retaliation, you might be misguided, at best, and a communist, at worst. This posture may also manifest itself in opposition to our Constitution, the Bill of Rights, natural law, God-given liberties, and the American republic. If these symptoms are present and the reader rejects the socialist label, then it is highly recommended that the reader take a harder look in the mirror and educate oneself with our founding documents and true history.

Reading this diagnosis, one may wrongly conclude that the author is disenfranchised with his fellow citizens, or that he is against the American populous. Nothing could be further from the truth. I stand for the American people. I want what is best for them and our great nation. I believe we should put our men and women in the military on a pedestal, as they have committed their lives to protect our freedoms, selflessly doing what many cannot or will not do. I am thankful for the first responders, firemen, police, and paramedics who come to our aid at the time of an emergency. I am grateful for the nurses and doctors who care for us when we are most vulnerable. I appreciate the good teachers and coaches who educate and help to instill proper values in our children. I am for the honest Americans who wish to live their lives in peace, work hard, obey laws, and strive for a better future for themselves and all generations hereafter.

I am, however, against the government bureaucrats, lobbyists, corporate fat cats, and other exploiters of the system who have lined their pockets with ill-gotten gains or have usurped power from the masses, and those who foster a culture of mediocrity, hide maleficence, and accept the poisoning of our nation. I am also against the cultural scourge that has blanketed our society like a choking smog.

I am a firm believer in a free marketplace obeying the laws of supply and demand and merit-based growth aimed at individual achievement. A flourishing meritocracy is a much better system for the people than a system where everybody gets the same handout. I am also against kakistocracy, our existing form of government: the state or society where the people are governed by its least-suitable or least-competent citizens.

The self-proclaimed "New World Order" protagonists will state that they know what is best for America. If granted, their extremist views will put us all into Orwellian shackles. Like Orwell's Boxer from *Animal Farm*, are we destined to be tethered to the iron plow tempered from our own years of ignorance, working until we fatally collapse, or will we shed this restraint? Are complacency and ignorance the outcomes we wish for future generations? I say not. We can no longer be complacent.

To shift the tide, we must stop playing defense and go on the offensive. Through a displayed allegiance, we must root out all that is truly "anti-American." Americans can no longer avoid common sense and courage. There are those who are trying to enslave us, but first they must divide us. By separating us back into tribes, they can alter the truth and pit us against each other. To regain our unity in a house divided, we must demand a state of truth in lieu of seeking fault. Only through a Second Revolution can we dare to shift the tide of power back to the rightful owners, *We the People*.

I challenge you to reject what you know in your heart is wrong, untrue, or unjust. Rebel against those wanting to divide us. Seek commonality, forgiveness, gratitude, and love toward your fellow citizens. None of what I preach will come without sacrifice and pain, yet rest easy in the knowledge that the American republic is worthy of the struggle.

It's Not Just
a Piece of Cloth

We take the stars from heaven, the red from
our mother country, separating it by white
stripes, thus showing that we have separated
from her, and the white stripes shall go down
to posterity representing Liberty.

—GEORGE WASHINGTON

May the Stars and Stripes always remain a symbol of freedom. Old Glory is not just a piece of cloth or an ornament for display. For many, it is a source of pride. For some, it is a target; for others, it represents sacrifice. The United States flag, an emblem of our great country, has evolved over time. An enduring symbol of strength that may fade, become worn, and even get a little torn, but it will not run. A representation of liberty and justice, it should be handled and displayed with the utmost care and respect.

The fifty stars on the flag represent the fifty United States. The thirteen stripes represent the Thirteen Colonies that declared independence from Great Britain and became the first states in the United States of America. According to custom and tradition, white signifies purity and innocence; red represents hardiness and valor; blue signifies vigilance, perseverance, and justice. According to Elizabeth Griscom Ross: "Stars on a field of blue; one for each colony; bars of red, for the blood of sacrifice; on a ground of white for love and peace."

Over recent decades, we have allowed the minority few to lessen her appeal. Decades ago, as students, we helped to raise and lower the flag in front of our school. We were taught to properly fold and handle the flag, and we stated the Pledge of Allegiance at the beginning of each day. Today, in order to avoid hurting someone's feelings, we diminish the very symbol that millions have faithfully given their lives to protect. It seems that most cannot be bothered to offer a simple oath or learn a few bars of our anthem. Sadly, by doing so, we fail to honor those men and women who believed our banner was worth dying for.

Today, many classrooms fail to recite the Pledge of Allegiance or sing "The Star-Spangled Banner," our national anthem. Regrettably, most students (and some adults) cannot state with any certainty the origins of either pledge. For the curious few, I offer the following reminder.

In August 1892, Francis Bellamy authored the Pledge of Allegiance: "I pledge allegiance to my Flag and the Republic for which it stands, one nation, indivisible, with liberty and justice for all." In its original form, citizens of any nation could have used Bellamy's pledge. Over time, the pledge was amended on multiple occasions until 1954, when the following version was adopted: "I pledge allegiance to the flag of the United States of America, and to the republic for which it stands, one nation under God, indivisible, with liberty and justice for all." I wish to remind the reader that those who seek to divide us have undermined this simple pledge to our flag.

Our national anthem stemmed from a poem penned by Francis Scott Key after witnessing the British Royal Navy bombardment of Fort McHenry during the War of 1812. Inspired by "The Star-Spangled Banner" that flew triumphantly above the fort during the U.S. victory, Key summarized his pride for our flag and the tenacity of our fledgling nation.

O say can you see, by the dawn's early light,
What so proudly we hail'd at the twilight's last gleaming,
Whose broad stripes and bright stars through the perilous fight
O'er the ramparts we watch'd were so gallantly streaming?
And the rocket's red glare, the bomb bursting in air,
Gave proof through the night that our flag was still there,
O say does that star-spangled banner yet wave
O'er the land of the free and the home of the brave?

For most Americans, the reciting of these lyrics brings a heartfelt swell of pride to one's chest and mist to the eyes. Regrettably, to the contrary, some see red, have a spontaneous desire to desecrate this symbol, and/or choose to kneel in protest. While many look upon this symbol with the utmost reverence, others are well within their rights to disrespect this national banner. Thankfully, we live in a country with a First Amendment, which protects this act of symbolic speech. For those who display contempt for our flag, you are within your rights. However, please remember two important facts: First, many Americans have served, fought, and even died to protect your right to disrespect our nation's flag. Second, in some foreign regimes, your defiant behavior would not be tolerated. Such an act of disrespect may seem cool here in the United States, but doing so in other less tolerant nations might result in you and your family being hauled off, never to be seen again. Be grateful that you rest at night under the protection of liberty that was stitched together with the tattered remnants from those who sacrificed all for our freedom.

Finally, let this serve as a reminder: As a citizen of this country, you are always basking under the freedoms and protections afforded to all of us while that red, white, and blue banner gallantly streams over our land. In the Second Revolution, I invite all Americans to find the courage to proudly display and stand up for our flag. With unabashed gratitude, please honor and respect this symbol of the American republic. Choosing not to will be an affront to all those brave Americans who endured the incredible hardships of war to protect our freedoms.

The American Dream

And if the American Dream is to be a reality,
we must continue to engage in creative
protests in order to break down those barriers
which make it impossible for us to realize the
American Dream.

—MARTIN LUTHER KING, JR.

The American Dream formed long before the creation of our nation when our Founding Fathers debated and penned the Declaration of Independence. The concept of a new beginning arrived with the earliest settlers. It was ultimately cemented when colonists put their lives at risk for the chance to obtain their goals and freedom. The American Dream emerged from our original pursuit of happiness. It remains today, somewhat battered and sullen, but this symbol of hope and freedom has not been beaten.

There have been many elites, celebrities, professors, so-called journalists, and cynics who have said that the American Dream is a false reality, that it is not available to all and is racist and should be discarded. Over the last few decades, this falsehood has been propagated in our classrooms, starting at the elementary level, and carried seamlessly through our higher education system. The systematic poisoning of a generation of minds with thoughts of oppression and victim mentality has been faithfully orchestrated within America. What these naysayers fail to recognize is the fact that freedom is a seed that is planted in all of us with hope being the only germination required. With a little love, encouragement, and optimism, the American Dream will never die.

It is this author's opinion that the American Dream is a mindset. It is the difference between a scarcity mentality and an abundance mentality. It is not about what we have or what we gain, or the trappings in life. Nor is it about trinkets we acquire or the assets we accumulate. The American Dream is tied to autonomy, freedom of choice, and our ability to exercise free will. To be human is to be free. All humans should long for freedom, like a newborn unencumbered by the demands of our world.

The American Dream requires hard work and grit. At times, it means making sacrifices or assuming additional risk. Sometimes there is an element of luck. The American Dream starts with the realization that it is possible. And for those who have been told otherwise, there is nothing to be ashamed of. The seed of the American Dream exists for all who yearn for a better future. One must dare to struggle, risk failure, and strive to achieve one's ideal to its fullest potential—none of which is guaranteed success. But like any seed, over time it must be watered, nurtured, and cultivated.

I would argue that elements of the American Dream exist for all of us and, despite all those who sigh in disgust when this belief is mentioned, the land of opportunity is alive and well. For most, the American Dream may be about achieving life goals, owning a home, or finding security. For some, it may mean becoming an entrepreneur and starting your own business. It may look more like a proud parent who has raised a family and provided for their children in ways that their parents were unable. It may take shape in the form of a career spent serving others or our nation in uniform. It may be realized in one's spare time directed toward helping others and giving back within their community. It can be someone who mastered a craft or skill and eventually passed it along as a mentor or coach. It might be the person who was happy to work for a good company for the majority of their working years, starting at the ground level and working their way through the ranks. It may come to pass for the individual who grew up on the East Coast and always wanted to perform music and live on the West Coast. Or it may befall on the person who was at the right place at the right time.

Ultimately, the American Dream is as individualized as we are individuals; there is no one formula or singular result. It does require a positive attitude, the willingness to tackle any job with dignity, and some "can-do" spirit. Very few of us have been born with a silver spoon in our mouths. However, the majority of all Americans have all experienced some sort of struggle, challenge, or setback. How we overcome these adversities with a positive attitude, grit, and determination is a form of the American Dream. Failure, achievement, and success require purposeful accomplishments, which all aid us in striving for our pursuit of happiness.

No country should be placed upon a pedestal as an exemplary model, yet I do believe there is an element of American exceptionalism within her history. While she has been a force for good, she has also had her share of unfortunate mishaps and intentional missteps. America, like the humans who inhabit her, is flawed. She draws her strength through our unity, hard work, ingenuity, steadfastness, and our belief in a higher power. Not the power that is shaped from greed, corruption, and the misgivings of others, but the power ordained to her by God.

America was founded as a more perfect union, a deterrent of evil and a protector of individual rights and freedoms. Some believe she is blessed by God's grace. While we have strayed at times from these good works, America has been and remains a symbol of hope for many around the world. Offered in a sermon long before she became the United States of America, the proclamation that "we shall be as a city upon a hill"[29] forecasted our manifest destiny.

President Ronald Reagan again put the hope of America up as a symbol for all to see. His powerful articulation of America's journey and light of hope for all the world to see, "a shining city on the hill,"[30] America continues to be a beacon and magnet for all those who seek freedom and a better life for themselves. This is witnessed in the generations that have migrated to this country since before its founding. If this was a false reality, why else would millions of immigrants walk hundreds of miles to cross our Southern border? The uniqueness of her offerings and limitless opportunities exists for all those fortunate enough to grace her lands.

No place else in the world are the masses drawn to more than America. What other country calls to people seeking freedom and opportunity? Look no farther than New York Harbor, where for decades immigrants from all across the seas landed with tears and a hope for a better future. The American Dream is a beacon to millions. Emma Lazarus artfully summed it up within her sonnet entitled, "The New Colossus," which adorns the Statue of Liberty.

> Give me your tired, your poor,
> Your huddled masses yearning to breathe free,
> The wretched refuse of your teeming shore.
> Send these, the homeless, tempest-tost to me,
> I lift my lamp beside the golden door!

Sadly, along the way we closed the golden door and left the back door open and unattended. During the era of Ellis Island, we processed more than twelve million immigrants. Not all arriving to our shores were accepted, and many were denied entry into the United States. Today, we dishonor those who entered legally, and we openly allow many of whom should be denied. Within the millions of recent immigrants who are also seeking the American Dream, there are many good people with hope in their eyes. Regretfully, however, there is an unknown amount that wishes us and America harm. For these unsavory masses, a gated entry is required.

More than anything, at the center of the American Dream is the hope for a better life. It is not racist to seek liberty from tyranny or want for a better future for oneself and one's family. Hope is the optimistic expectation for a better outcome. These ideals should be coveted, celebrated, and not cast aside. This dream should not be robbed from our children. In fact, we should want this for all of mankind.

From the beginning, the reader should note that the American government is not the shining beacon. It is the hope of America that invokes this dream. We, the grateful citizens of this fine republic, shall never stop fighting for the American Dream and our blessed way of life. Thomas Paine warns, "Those who expect to reap the blessings of freedom must, like men, undergo the fatigue of supporting it."[31] It is our responsibility to support the republic through our willingness to defend her ideals in the coming Second Revolution. We each have a choice in our future. We can either choose to move toward a better future or continue on our path of regression.

A Call
to Action

*The tree of liberty must be refreshed from time
to time with the blood of patriots and tyrants.
It is its natural manure.*

—THOMAS JEFFERSON

I call upon you, as fellow citizens, to help raise up our communities and the America that we deserve. Political and racial lines are only enforced by those who seek to separate us. Put an end to this unrest. Reject the polarization and discord that has been thrust upon us. Have a civil discussion, truly seek first to understand, then work to effect change and move together as a united front. At one point in our society, we were able to disagree and accept that we are not all the same.

I implore the reader to expect and demand more from our elected representatives and so-called leaders. Mandate that they uphold the laws of the land, our ideals, and insist that they cast away the cynics and the snakes with their overt and blatant disregard for American values, rights, and liberties.

Our leaders should be successful but proven business and servant leaders. They must be purposeful and selfless leaders who steward the best interests of the American people and our republic above anything else. Servant citizens who step forward into the arena and fight for the natural rights of the American people in support of life, liberty, and the pursuit of happiness.

No different than a chief executive officer assuming his or her role at the helm of a failing company, or a surgeon standing over an ailing patient, our future leaders should step into office with their eyes wide open. Knowing to expect the unexpected, they shall be ready to make the difficult decisions required to save the republic. Upon assessing the current conditions on the ground, our leaders should act decisively and intentionally, like a surgeon removing a cancerous tumor, cutting waste, eliminating redundancy, and removing any malignancies from our diseased bureaucracy.

Our America requires immediate full triage, and failing to treat the decay that has befallen her will only lead to a complete demise of our liberties. Listed below are a few actions that I believe should be considered and/or implemented immediately. More may come to light as treatment progresses, yet these urgent actions are essential to save the American republic.

* Reduce the size of government, eliminate ineffective and corrupt agencies, and cut back the bloated bureaucratic kudzu. Institute an immediate federal government hiring freeze, and implement an incremental reduction of its workforce and spending budgets.
* Return to the intended framework of our Constitution and the Bill of Rights, and stop infringing upon our rights.
* Require term limits for *all* state and federal government positions, elected and appointed.
* Work within a balanced budget, and add a balanced budget provision to the U.S. Constitution.
* Eliminate government handouts, but provide provide a temporary safety net for those who truly need it, yet end all wasteful programs.

* Stop devaluing our currency, and move us
  back to the gold standard.
* Depart from needless, wasteful spending,
  and live within our means.
* Simplify the tax code by establishing a
  flat income tax that we all equally pay, no
  matter the income level or our position
  in life.
* Reestablish our energy independence,
  including the development of future
  sources of alternative energy.
* Secure our border, and establish a fair and
  effective immigration policy.
* Take care of our veterans as well as the
  men and women actively serving within
  our military.
* Obtain peace through strength by readying
  our military for all threats, foreign and
  domestic.
* Stop meddling in global affairs that do not
  directly impact our national interests.
* Promote a pro-business philosophy, and
  reduce unwarranted regulations in support
  of the millions of small businesses.
* Stop embracing Modern Monetary
  Theory or applying nonfinancial factors,
  such as woke environmental, social, and

governance (ESG) to investing and/or corporate governance.

★ Bring back (onshore) our critical manufacturing.

★ Eliminate executive orders, and follow the established rules set forth within the Constitution and the Bill of Rights.

★ Establish a Parents Bill of Rights with the sole purpose of protecting our children.

★ Stop lowering the educational bar and return to a traditional curriculum. In addition to focusing on reading, writing, history (an unaltered version), and STEM classes, go back to teaching life skills and skilled trades.

★ Similar to rules regarding smoking, alcohol, and driving, etc., establish strict age limits and restrict access to social media platforms.

★ Hold the tech oligarchies accountable by revoking protections under Section 230 of the Constitution.

★ Eliminate lobbying and lobbyists.

★ Restore the integrity of our elections. Free and fair, with consistent results presented on election day, free of all political hijinks and dark money.

* Reestablish law and order. Uphold the laws of our land, adhere to one standard form of justice, and reform the criminal justice system.

* Repeal all laws and provisions that conflict or are contrary to the original intent and structure of the constitution while ensuring that power remains in the peoples' hands.

* Stop with the anti-carbon cult agenda. We can do good works to protect our planet and environment without poisoning the existence for future generations. Remember, every element of our human body and all known living things embody chains of carbon atoms.

* Protect the sanctity of all human life by eliminating the senseless killings in our society, to ending the suffering and decay in our streets by stopping the scourge of human trafficking and respecting the lives of the unborn. All life is a sacred gift that should be honored and celebrated. All life matters.

* Rebuild our mental health network in support of our homeless community.

* Restore trust in our government institutions.

* Institute a federal government hiring freeze across all agencies, and implement an incremental reduction of its workforce and related budgets. Start with a minimum of 25 percent, and include the termination of all associated lifelong employee benefits.
* Disband the federal government employees' union. Its existence is unconstitutional, as they cannot be removed by the executive branch.
* Stop with the *rules for thee and not for me.* Elected representatives shall be held to the same standards as their electors. Stop with the self-gratification and the accumulation of power and personal wealth at the expense of your constituents.
* Hold accountable those elected representatives and government officials who have been found guilty of portraying illegal acts against the American people.

Finally, elected leaders, remember that you are an elected representative government working for the American people. We do not work for you!

Like Paine, I am promoting a revolution, yet I must be very clear that I am not fomenting violence or asking my fellow countrymen to take up arms. I am, however, seeking a peaceful return to common sense and competent leadership.

I am hopeful that a strong wind of revolution will clear the air, allowing Americans to once again catch a glimpse of her full potential. I am hopeful that enough Americans will regain common sense and will demand that our American principles and values be upheld. Finally, I am hopeful that our Founding Fathers' revolution and struggle for our freedoms was not in vain.

I have great empathy for the American people and their struggle. I wish them only the best in this life and in the lives of future generations. It's time to take back our country and its cultural institutions, wiping clean the progressive agenda that has infiltrated our republic. I am ready to stand inspired alongside my fellow countrymen in our Second Revolution for freedom.

I am hopeful that the sleeping giant of the American populous will once again awaken. However, beyond being stirred from our slumber, we must take action. If you are reading this and agree with its merits, I respectfully ask that you consider the following four demands.

One, please share this book with a family member, friend, neighbor, or a coworker who may be disengaged or may have a differing viewpoint. Calmly discuss the merits and/or shortcomings of this narrative, find some commonality, and then build upon it.

Secondly, please get engaged in your local community; participate in your church or civic organization. Get involved in your school board, volunteer, and/or run for your local government. Please stand up for what you believe in and fight for the ideals of America.

Thirdly, please proudly display your patriotism, fly Old Glory, and celebrate the blessings of this nation. Do not capitulate to social pressures and stoke the flames of freedom. Have hope for America. Bring forward the belief that she was a divine gift to the world. Her ideals are meant for a better human existence, free of oppression or a dictator's rule.

Lastly, please vote for those representatives who will act on behalf of the American people, and send home those lifelong bureaucrats with self-serving interests. Please make sure your voice is heard. Show our elected representatives that they work for us, and we will oppose tyranny at all levels.

In the end, most Americans want the same things. We all want a better life for ourselves and our families, especially our children and grand-children. We want unity, equal opportunity, equal treatment under the law, and a healthy environment where we can all live. We want autonomy, purpose, and the ability to better ourselves and others around us. Most of all, we want hope for a brighter future. No matter your race, color, sex, religion, age, or nation of origin, if we want these truths to be self-evident, then *We the People* must stand together for America.

Restoring a Nation Through Revolution

Freedom is a fragile thing and it's never more
than one generation away from extinction.
It is not ours by way of inheritance;
it must be fought for and defended constantly
by each generation, for it comes only once to
a people. And those in world history who
have known freedom and then lost it have
never known it again.

—RONALD REAGAN

I feel unworthy and certainly ill-equipped to speak on theology, yet I feel called upon to wade into uncertain waters. I can no longer stand by and watch the destruction of God's creation. It pains me to see the erosion of natural law and the great blessings and opportunities that we are squandering through our inaction and complacency. However, that does not mean we can't change, but we must act swiftly and with intention.

We must, as a collective society, rebel against the evil forces in play against Americans. It is time for America's Second Revolution.

The revolution of which I speak is not a call to violence. In fact, quite the opposite. Bloodshed only illustrates our ignorance. Furthermore, patriots shouldn't fear, as societies' false prophets will not act to shed the blood of their family, neighbors, and fellow comrades over hollow ideals. If brought to bear, our strength—which derives from our commonality, goodness, and the favor of Mother America and God—can overwhelm the evil usurping our liberties. I pray, absent of bloodshed, that the moral pendulum will soon swing back toward normalcy and truer American virtues to include the restoration of Judeo-Christian values. However, this shift will not occur without countrymen stepping up bravely to restrain the sickly momentum for which we now swing.

I hold no moral authority or theological credentials, yet I call loudly, with the hope of stir-ring a much-needed spiritual awakening. Peace and prosperity can be attained though nobler means. Our freedom, framework, and flag were all based on the simple teachings of the Lord and His glory. Straying from God's basic tenants has led us to be a nation and society in moral decline.

Only our Creator's divine authority and wisdom can restore us to our proper standing.

O ye of little faith and abject dissenters . . . you may shrink away from this prognosis, yet I hope the Second Revolution, a spiritual awakening, will soon come. It will arise with a groundswell of faith and the belief in a better America. And, for those who may twist my words, let me state this clearly: I am not inciting violence. I speak of revolution, not revolt. However, do not misjudge my intentions. I am not advocating to turn one's cheek away from evil. To the contrary, we must root out all evil from our society. We can do so through truth, forgiveness, and love. Light, through truth, is the only antiseptic. Truth, not fear or violence, shall be our only savior.

The next American Revolution should be founded on faith and tradition. What if the Second Coming of Jesus Christ is not about us waiting for Him and looking forward to His arrival, but the masses going to Him through our rejuvenated faith? This vision may strike many as odd or even blasphemous, yet can we afford to wait? Maybe the only way to subdue the division among us is through a present-day resurrection.

Trepidation in one's heart will be a force multiplier against those forsaken. We must act now. The longer we delay, the less likely a correction can be achieved. And once the Rubicon is crossed, the fate of future generations will be sealed. Understand fully that current citizens of our republic will not pay the ultimate price for our complacency; it will be future generations who will receive the toll. For our lackadaisical attitude toward the gift that was bestowed upon us almost a quarter of a century ago will not go unpunished.

The natural rights of future generations should rightly not be denied as a result of our inaction. Doing nothing is akin to parents willingly placing shackles about the hands, feet, and souls of their children. Historians will have it correct if they blame us for the worst form of heresy against the world. This egregious crime and the blood of the innocent will be on our hands. If the republic does perish, then it will be at the hands of *We the People*. It would mean that we were unable to awaken from our impaired stupor.

Therefore, do not fall prey to neurotic virtue signaling, falsehoods, or politically motivated agendas. Suppress any desire to shy away from spreading the truth when faced with these malevolent attacks. If we waver, the anti-American agenda will ultimately win, and evil will triumph. "Iron sharpens iron,"[32] one's resolve strengthens another's, and together *We the People* can prevail. Our dependence upon each other is the only avenue to independence. Thus, being willing to declare that while we may not agree on everything, it doesn't preclude us from working together for a better future. Remember, "Forgiveness means letting go of the hope for a better past."[33]

Scripture says, "But I say to you, love your enemies, bless those who curse you, do good to those who spitefully use you and persecute you."[34] While hope for a better future is needed, it is not the only bridge that will deliver us to the outcome we desire. Through actions that benefit others, we can disarm our enemies and keep their lies and hatred at bay. By living lives of gratitude and forgiveness, we can narrow the expanse. With stiffened resolve, goodness in our hearts, rekindled faith, and unconditional love for each other, we can prevail. In the sincerest form of union inherent with our motto, "E Pluribus Unum," all faiths that peacefully serve mankind are welcome. Seek unity and we shall find peace.

Some may say that the prescribed pathway is too steep and insurmountable to overcome. The reader is reminded that change worth longing for will not come overnight, so do not be discouraged.

Durable change will come slowly, yet it should not be mistaken for inaction.

Others may claim that the journey is not worth the effort and others can bear the burden. If you are expecting improvement without action, then you are no more than a fool. Stop deceiving yourself. If you remain passive, you shall be like sheep led to the slaughter. If one waits for sorrow to be delivered to one's doorstep to act, it will be much too late. Inaction will enslave future generations, and doing so is unacceptable as we can no longer surrender to the ways of evil.

Sadly, some may even say America is a lost cause. Even if a fraction of this claim may be true, isn't America not worth fighting for? I submit yes, she is. Furthermore, all freedom-loving Americans must stop with the apologetic appeasement and accommodation of anti-American rhetoric. Stand steadfast in your faith in the American spirit and resolve, and the good citizens of the republic shall prevail.

Yes, "THESE are the times that try men's souls. The summer soldier and the sunshine patriot will, in this crisis, shrink from the service of their country; but he that stands by it now, deserves the love and thanks of man and woman. Tyranny, like hell, is not easily conquered; yet we have this consolation with us, that the harder the conflict, the more glorious the triumph."[35]

How does the individual pierce the armor of the government shield? One cannot alone, yet together, *We the People* can. But how? The answer is simple and can be achieved in mere moments. Our full faith is required, as the Almighty will not fight our battles unless we are willing to stand and fight alongside Him. Only God (not government) has divine authority over this land and her inhabitants. "The sun never shined on a cause of greater worth."[36] Life, liberty, and the favor of America is in our hands. Go forth and bring God's influence to bear as together we shall vanquish those who have stained the soul of America.

It is time to wake up, America! Rise from the slumber of this nightmarish decline, and take action to save this great nation. Rise up against the anti-American plague. Act by standing firm in your faith and within your spirit by serving our republic.

* Serve the republic by rooting out the zealots who are bent for communism and absolute power.
* Serve the community by giving freely, contributing your time, energy, and knowledge.

* Serve those who may differ in thought by engaging in open, thorough, and thoughtful debate, challenging all false narratives by speaking the truth.
* Serve your family, friends, and neighbors by spreading joy, gratitude, hope, and love.
* Serve yourself by eliminating those false facades that encumber you. Be authentic, and humbly go out into the world with the knowledge that you are worthy. Through faith and love, pursue happiness.
* Serve the future by protecting our children, ensuring that they are no longer victimized, brainwashed, or indoctrinated during their formative years.
* Serve your enemies by differentiating between pure evil and those who are just disagreeable. We should turn the other cheek when approached by the latter; whereas pure evil must be deterred from a forward-facing opposition.
* Finally, serve your Creator by honoring the many blessings He has bestowed upon us, our nation, and our world. Those who are righteous and do these things are the salt, the light, and the blessed of the earth.

In his 1910 speech, Theodore Roosevelt reminds us of what is at stake for a "Citizenship in a Republic."[37]

It is not the critic who counts; not the man who points out how the strong man stumbles, or where the doer of deeds could have done them better. The credit belongs to the man who is actually in the arena, whose face is marred by dust and sweat and blood; who strives valiantly; who errs, who comes short again and again, because there is no effort without error and shortcoming; but who does actually strive to do the deeds; who knows the great enthusiasms, the great devotions; who spends himself in a worthy cause; who at the best knows in the end the triumph of high achievement, and who at the worst, if he fails, at least fails while daring greatly, so that his place shall never be with those cold and timid souls who neither know victory nor defeat. Shame on the man of cultivated taste who permits refinement to develop into fastidiousness that unfits him for doing the rough work of a workaday world. Among the free peoples who govern themselves there is but a small field of usefulness open for the men of cloistered life who shrink from contact with their fellows. Still less room is there for those who deride or slight what is done by those who actually bear the brunt of the day; nor yet for those others who always profess that they would like to take action, if only the conditions of life were not exactly what they actually are. The man who does nothing cuts the same sordid figure in the pages of history, whether he be cynic, or fop, or voluptuary. There is little use for the being whose tepid soul knows nothing of the great and generous emotion, of the high pride, the stern belief, the lofty enthusiasm, of the men who quell the storm and ride the thunder. Well for these men if they succeed; well also, though not so well, if they fail, given only that they have nobly ventured, and have put forth all their heart and strength.

Isn't it time to dare greatly and adhere to common sense? God's revolutionaries and fellow patriots must rise up to protect the republic. Look beyond petty differences and unite together as fellow countrymen. Work together to root out the evil in our world and pave the way for a better future. Stand firm against the headwinds of tyranny, and pray for those who are lost or are ignorant of what they do. Be Americans and honor God's glory and gift. Help to restore the shining "City on the Hill." Do these things **For Love of Country**.

Lastly, I would like to impart upon the reader a prayer for America written by General George Washington of the Continental Army.

Almighty God; We make our earnest prayer that Thou wilt keep the United States in Thy holy protection; that Thou wilt incline the hearts of the citizens to cultivate a spirit of subordination and obedience to government; and entertain a brotherly affection and love for one another and for their fellow citizens of the United States at large.

And finally that Thou wilt most graciously be pleased to dispose us all to do justice, to love mercy, and to demean ourselves with that charity, humility, and pacific temper of mind which were the characteristics of the Divine Author of our blessed religion, and without a humble imitation of whose example in these things we can never hope to be a happy nation. Grant our supplication, we beseech Thee, through Jesus Christ our Lord. Amen.

May God bless the people of our republic, and may God bless America.

Author's Note

> *That this nation under God, shall have a new birth of freedom, and that government of the people, by the people, for the people, shall not perish from the earth.*
>
> —ABRAHAM LINCOLN

Dear Reader,

I wanted to share with you a little more context behind the conclusion of this book. In writing this, I felt like one of the Lord's lost sheep being called upon to carry out His message. I personally feel unworthy to be so bold to make this claim as I have not been a righteous man or a religious person. Yes, I have much faith in a higher power, but I struggle, like many others, to understand. I am a simple man with an inquiring mind who is employing the skills and knowledge acquired over nearly six decades of life. I am, at best, a tarnished vessel carrying forth the Lord's will.

I recently heard someone say that they conflated God with man's organized religion. This statement resonated with me. From an early age, I have looked at religion as a creation of man; its benefits were only as good as the man delivering the message and the house of worship that was created for its delivery. I held little credence in the benefits of either.

Over time, my lack of knowledge about God, Jesus Christ, and His teachings have perplexed me. This lack of understanding, combined with my thirst for questioning and my travels around the world, especially to the Holy Land, have awakened a spiritual stirring within me. Maybe it is a confluence of age, life experiences, and wisdom, but I feel closer now to this still-untouchable object.

Ultimately, the world needs a force for peace, justice, and goodness. I believe that America was created to be this force, the shining City on the Hill. Regrettably, flawed men have ruled over her lands, and too many have used her to seek out personal gain. Some have lost their moral compass along the way; others were flat-out corrupt.

In the end, "the meek shall inherit the earth."[38] I believe that means the good people, seeking a simple life of joy, love, purpose, and gratitude, will eventually win the day. But first, we must rise up, unite, and rally together to defeat evil, educate the unknowing, and lead the misguided. Once again, the sleeping giant must be awakened. Americans, and global citizens around the world, if you truly want a better life for your children and future generations, it is time to coalesce.

May God bless us all,
Norman W. Holden

Acknowledgments

First, I would like to thank several friends and family members who took valuable time to provide feedback on earlier versions of my manuscript. I intentionally asked people who were center, left, and right in their political thinking, as I wanted *For Love of Country* to resonate with all Americans. Thank you, Jennifer, Kathleen, Lloyd, Michelle, and Owen, for your words of wisdom.

I would also like to thank Jenna and Sarah for their editorial and design work respectively. This is our third project together, and I truly appreciate your professionalism and support.

Last and most important, I especially want to thank my wife, Jean, for her patience, guidance, and love while I struggled with several drafts of this book. I know you would like for me to be more succinct with my writing, yet what can I say. I love you!

About the Author

A twelfth-generation American, Norman W. Holden was born and raised in one of the original colonies, the "Live Free or Die" state of New Hampshire. Growing up with the engrained understanding that freedom is not free and surrounded by our early colonial history, Norm was taught from an early age to respect and honor our country, our flag, and our closely held traditions. Norm is the author of *Do Better!* and *The Lucky Seven* and is an executive leader in the construction industry. Norm resides in Conifer, Colorado, with his wife, Jean.

Dear Reader,

If you enjoyed my book and would like to read more of my stories, you can help me in three ways: please leave a review on Amazon, or at the online store you purchased from; spread the word to family and friends and on social media; and visit my website at https://normanholdenbooks.com/ by scanning the QR code below. Once there, please join my mailing list and learn about future releases and other news related to my books.

I appreciate your support,
Norman W. Holden

References

Bartlett, J. (1948). *Familiar Quotations*. Boston, MA: Little, Brown and Company.

Marx, K., & Engels, F. (1888). *The Communist Manifesto*. London.

New King James Version. (2020). *The Holy Bible*. Nashville, TN: Thomas Nelson.

Paine, T. (1776). *Common Sense*. Philadelphia, PA: Anonymous.

Paine, T. (1776). *The Crisis*. Philadelphia, PA: Anonymous.

The Constitution of the United States of America and Selected Writings of The Founding Fathers (2012). New York, NY: Barnes & Noble.

Endnotes

Preface

1   Part of a speech given by E.H. Heywood in Boston, Massachusetts, on November 16, 1862, which later became a children's rhyme.

2   Taken from a line in "America the Beautiful," the patriotic song written by Katharine Lee Bates (1893).

A House Divided

3   Quote attributed to Will Durant from his 1926 book *The Story of Philosophy*.

4   The Bible, New King James version, Matthew 12:22–28.

5   Introduction opening paragraph from Thomas Paine's *Common Sense*, (1776).

6   Paine, *Common Sense*, (1776).

7   Paine, *Common Sense*, (1776).

We the People

8   https://www.whitehouse.gov/about-the-white-house/our-government/the-constitution/

9   Preamble to the United States Constitution – On June 22, 1787, New Hampshire became the ninth

State to ratify, which triggered the three-fourths rule. Subsequently, the Confederation Congress established March 9, 1789, as the date to begin operating under the Constitution.

10   Ratified on December 15, 1791.

11   Written in 1748 by Charles-Louis de Secondat, baron de La Brède et de Montesquieu, a French political philosopher.

A Threat to Democracy

12   This quote is often attributed to Aristotle yet is apocryphal and its origins are unknown.

The Threat Among Us

13   An excerpt from *The Life of Reason: The Phases of Human Progress*, (1905).

14   Marx & Engels, (1888).

15   Quote attributed to Joseph Stalin and Joseph Goebbels.

16   Marxist theories were influential in the development of socialism.

17   From Thomas Jefferson in a 1787 letter to William S. Smith.

Sovereignty Matters

18   James Warren Jones, better known as Jim Jones, was an American preacher who, with his inner

circle, led the members of the Peoples Temple and orchestrated a mass murder-suicide in his remote jungle commune at Jonestown, Guyana, on November 18, 1978, killing over 900 commune members with cyanide-laced Flavor Aid.

19   *Two Treatises of Government*, published in 1689.

Taxation Without Representation

20   James Otis, a firebrand lawyer, and Massachusetts representative had popularized the phrase "taxation without representation is tyranny" in a series of public arguments.

21   Refer to www.usdebtclock.org for the latest figures.

Don't Tread on Me

22   A phrase coined in 1904 by the American writer O. Henry.

23   Most sources simply call this an ancient proverb of unknown origin. Some speculate that it came from the Greeks, the Chinese, or the Turks originally. However, there is no definitive proof.

24   Written in a letter from Lord Action to Bishop Creighton.

25   Marx & Engels, (1888).

26   Marx & Engels, (1888).

27   A novella published in August 1945.

28   A science fiction novel published in June 1949.

The American Dream

29   A 1630 sermon by John Winthrop.

30   From the "Farewell Address to the Nation," delivered on January 11, 1989.

31   An excerpt from *The American Crisis*, 1777.

Restoring a Nation Through Revolution

32   The Bible, New King James version, Proverbs 27:17.

33   Attributed to Lama Surya Das.

34   The Bible, New King James version, Matthew 5:43–44.

35   Paine, *The Crisis*, (1776).

36   Paine, *Common Sense*, (1776).

37   Speech entitled "Citizenship in a Republic" delivered at the Sorbonne in Paris on April 23, 1910.

Author's Note

38   The Bible, New King James version, Psalms 37:11.

Printed in the USA
CPSIA information can be obtained
at www.ICGtesting.com
LVHW050216140224
771728LV00007B/468/J